A
Girlfriend
Is a
Sister You
Choose

Edited by
Angela Joshi

Blue Mountain Press™
Boulder, Colorado

We gratefully acknowledge the permission granted by the following authors, publishers, and authors' representatives to reprint poems or excerpts from their publications: Susan Polis Schutz for "There is no need for...." Copyright © 1976 by Continental Publications, renewed © 2002 by Stephen Schutz and Susan Polis Schutz. And for "A friend is an extension...," "Our friendship does not depend...," and "We have formed a friendship...." Copyright © 1980, 1982, 1983 by Stephen Schutz and Susan Polis Schutz. All rights reserved. PrimaDonna Entertainment Corp. for "A Girlfriend Is a Sister You Choose" and "Girlfriends Keep Us Sane" by Donna Fargo. Copyright © 2006 by PrimaDonna Entertainment Corp. All rights reserved. Da Capo/Marlowe & Co., a member of Perseus Book Group, for "A girlfriend is beauty and grace..." by Christy Rosché and "A true girlfriend means something" and "Whether we manage children..." by Annette Annechild, PhD from I CAN TELL HER ANYTHING: THE POWER OF GIRL TALK by Annette Annechild, PhD. Copyright © 2005 by Annette Annechild. All rights reserved. Grand Central Publishing for "Friends are people who reflect..." from TEN THINGS I WISH I'D KNOWN BEFORE I WENT OUT INTO THE REAL WORLD by Maria Shriver. Copyright © 2000 by Maria Shriver. Reprinted by permission of Grand Central Publishing. All rights reserved. Cynthia Niswonger for "Some sisters are born...." Copyright © 2010 by Cynthia Niswonger. All rights reserved. John Wiley and Sons, Inc., for "My friends are my family," and "In spite of all the things..." by Oprah Winfrey and "She was there when..." by Gayle King from OPRAH WINFREY SPEAKS by Janet Lowe. Copyright © 1998 by Janet Lowe. All rights reserved. Joan Lunden Productions, www.joanlunden.com, for "Friends... allow us to savor our successes..." from WAKE-UP CALLS: MAKING THE MOST OF EVERY DAY by Joan Lunden. Copyright © 2001 by New Life Entertainment, Inc. All rights reserved.

Acknowledgments are continued on the last page.

Library of Congress Control Number: 2009913635
ISBN: 978-1-59842-487-4

Blue Mountain Arts, Inc.

P.O. Box 4549, Boulder, Colorado 80306

Contents

(Authors listed in order of first appearance)

A Girlfriend
Is a Sister You Choose

Girlfriends walk through life together, whether they live close or far apart. They know that the other one is there... to share the highs and the lows and everything else. They are connected at the heart, and their commitment to their friendship is permanent. They believe in each other. They are sensitive and supportive, and they can talk about things they may not even talk to their families about. Each of them knows the other will understand, no matter what.

Girlfriends aren't afraid to break the rules,
defend each other, and go out of their way.
They've cried together and laughed together,
and they have been there when it mattered.
Their loyalty is strong and lasting, and their
bond is unquestionable and unconditional.
They know that they'll keep on being there
through everything life has in store for them.

No one can take the place of a girlfriend, just
like no one can take your place in my life. You
will always live in my heart... just like family.

■ Donna Fargo

You're an Amazing Friend
...and an Amazing Person

You are so good to the people in your life —
so considerate and caring. When you give,
it's easy to see that it comes straight from the
heart... and it gives everyone around you the
gift of a nicer world to live in.

I love how strong you are inside. I always see
that quality shine in you, and it reassures me
to know — even though you face hardships and
uncertainties just like many people do — there's
a way through and a brighter day ahead. You're
my reminder to be a little more brave, to not
be so afraid, and to remember that things will
turn out okay in the long run.

I love the way you don't let the crazy, difficult days get you down. I admire your ability to put things in perspective — to laugh when you can, to cry when you must, but always to try to make things better.

I hope you'll never forget how much I treasure just being in this world with you. You are everything a friend should be. And I really hope that all your days are as beautiful and as bright... as the ones you inspire in other people's lives.

Lorrie Westfall

What Is a Girlfriend?

A girlfriend is one of
life's most beautiful gifts.

■ Luann Auciello

A girlfriend is beauty and grace with
arms outstretched to support and serve.
She is love and honor, and laughter
with smiles. Her friendship is easy and
uncomplicated. Flowing around and over
you, her spirit protects you. And she
listens. A true girlfriend listens to your
heart and opens your soul. You trust
her and in that trust you are connected....
A true girlfriend is an honor to have
and a pleasure to be.

■ Christy Rosché

$\mathcal{F}$riends are people who reflect different aspects and interests of your life. For me, there are the other mothers, the work partners, the diet buddies, the gossip hounds, the soul sisters. It's a handpicked support network tailor-made by me for me — especially important since I have no biological sisters. They help me with the kids, tell me I don't have to be Superwoman, warn me if I'm not being true to myself, and scream that I don't have to lose another five pounds. Girlfriends are the ones who fill in the gaps and pick up the slack left by your primary relationship. That's what friends are for.

◼ Maria Shriver

$\mathcal{A}$ friend is an extension of yourself without which you are not complete.

◼ Susan Polis Schutz

We're More Than Friends

Some sisters are born into our families to share triumphs, hurts, and losses along with Mom's cooking. They are there when we learn how to ride a bike, walk in heels, or get braces. They know every scar on our bodies and wound in our hearts, because they were there to see them formed.

Then there are the sisters who come along later in our lives and fall quietly into step, learning all the words and stories as if they'd always been there. We don't always see these sisters coming; often we look up when we are lost or in need to suddenly find them there. Just when we think we can't go on, they are the ones who step in and hold us up. They cheer us on and hold our hands, believing in us and all we do and loving us as if they'd always been a part of our lives.

■ Cynthia Niswonger

My friends are my family.

■ Oprah Winfrey

Friends... allow us to savor our
successes and our joys, comfort us
in our challenging moments, and
provide a mirror for us to learn more
about ourselves. I've always looked
at friends as the family we choose.
They enrich our lives.

■ Joan Lunden

You Are My Sister in Everything but Name

It's not just that I can tell you anything — it's that I don't even have to speak and you understand me just the same.

We celebrate each other's triumphs gladly; share gossip, but don't really mean it; offer advice, whether or not it's wanted; provide fashion tips, book critiques, movie reviews, and more. We back each other up when it comes to the really important things — like whether or not to order dessert.

We've given and taken without keeping score, borrowed and bought and not kept track. We've been overscheduled and overwhelmed, and we've done too much for so many, but we always stay in touch.

You let me shine without dimming your own light. You let me be myself — however messy and crazy and difficult I can be at times.

You're in my past, present, and future — a part of my soul. For all the late-night chats, hysterical laughter, hugs, and tears we've shared... I celebrate our friendship always.

■ Carrie Stollings

We Were Destined to Be Friends

$\mathcal{I}$ believe some paths are meant to cross —
to meet at friendship's door,
to share life's moments
    in togetherness, gladness,
and caring for each other.
I believe some doors are meant to open —
to invite two people in,
to change two lives forever,
to brighten moments with laughter,
and to have a place that feels like home.
I believe a special plan
was designed to bring us together
so that you and I could share this life
    as friends.

■ Barbara J. Hall

When we first met,
I felt like I had known you all my life.
I could talk to you so easily,
trust you with my
    innermost thoughts,
and laugh with you on
    the spur of the moment.

With you as my friend,
I don't have to pretend to be
    anything I'm not.
You accept me for who I am.

You're that rare kind of person
who cares enough to allow
and even encourage others
    to be who they are.
It is hard to find the words
to adequately express how much
I appreciate our friendship.
It is one that will always be cherished.

■ Rita Lechlitner

Let's Never Let Go of Our Friendship

Our friendship does not depend
on being together
It is deeper than that
Our closeness is something
     inside of us
that is always there
ready to be shared with each other
whenever the need arises
It is such a warm and comfortable
     feeling
to know that
we have such a lifetime
friendship

■ Susan Polis Schutz

I don't ever want us to let go of each other. Maybe our paths will go in separate directions, but that won't change the bond we share and what's in our hearts.

No matter where I am or what I am doing, when you come to mind a smile comes to my face and a warmth settles in my heart.

The day you and I met will always be cherished. We've grown together, done a lot together, and no matter what, we always let each other know that we do love and care about each other.

You are more than just a friend to me. I know we'll never let go of what we share, because whether it's across the miles or just a short distance, you are and will always be a part of my life.

■ Betsy Gurganus

A True Friend

What makes someone feel like a true friend? I think it is the ease in communication, the feeling of not being afraid to trust someone with your heart and your most private feelings.

■ Diana Ross

A true girlfriend *means* something. She is the person you can call in the middle of the night, and no matter what, she will help you. You can tell her anything. When you are sad, scared, or confused, she is the person you can turn to for comfort, caring, and advice. She is a true girlfriend.

■ Annette Annechild, PhD

$\mathcal{A}$ true friend is someone who is there for you.... There have been a lot of ups, a lot of positive things in my life, but there are things that are not so fun to deal with. My friend hears about things from me, and a true friend is someone who listens to everything.

■ Miley Cyrus

$\mathcal{T}$rue friends are there to support you when you need it, and if they have an issue with your friendship, they'll bring it to your attention so you can discuss and resolve it. They'll defend your character even when you aren't there.... They'll come over to your house at midnight with ice cream after you've just broken up with your boyfriend, or bring you chicken soup and orange juice when you're sick. And they'll do these things without asking for anything in return other than your company and good conversation.

■ Mary Lou Retton

Girlfriends Trust
Each Other Completely

Some things are too important,
  too sensitive, too painful,
    too delicate
to be shared with the whole world.

Dreams, hopes, fears,
memories, fantasies, heart's desires...
These are soul secrets —
  sacred trusts —
safe only with a girlfriend
who will hold them gently
with love and respect
  in the confines of her heart.

Thank you for being my confidante,
  my trusted friend,
    my secret agent.

BJ Gallagher

$\mathcal{I}$ trust her with parts of myself I don't trust with anybody else, and I can be honest about confessing things to her — even when it doesn't feel good.... We never fight. Even when it gets icky, we just talk it out. She's blood. She's my chosen family.

■ Jennifer Aniston

When I am around my friends I feel *good*. I feel *secure*. Our friendship is based on something that is completely unspoken: trust. And that trust, combined with years of experiences together, has forged a bond of understanding and unconditional love.

■ Queen Latifah

We Can Talk
About Anything

Our friendship has always been the kind
    that lets us talk
and tell each other anything.
We've always gathered
    our thoughts and feelings
and laid them at each other's doorstep.
We've shared a million memories,
and we've opened those special places
    in the heart
where only good friends are welcome.
We've been open and honest
    with each other;
we've had the kind of friendship
    that most people never find.

■ Barbara J. Hall

𝒥alk is at the very heart of women's friendships, the core of the way women connect. It's the given, the absolute assumption of friendship....

When a friend calls with a serious problem while you're cooking dinner, the pot goes on the back burner. When something happens at work or home that you can't quite, exactly, figure out, you take all that raw undigested feeling to a safe place — a friend — and come away clearer.

■ Ellen Goodman and Patricia O'Brien

𝒻ew comforts are more alluring for a woman than the rich, intimate territory of women's talk. A woman friend will say, "You are not alone. I have felt that way, too. This is what happened to me." Home, in other words.

■ Elsa Walsh

Sometimes We Don't Need Words at All

One of the most beautiful qualities
of true friendship is to understand
and to be understood.

◼ Seneca

There is no need for
an outpouring of words
to explain oneself
to a friend
Friends understand
each other's thoughts
even before
they are spoken

◼ Susan Polis Schutz

Friends don't have to
talk all the time to stay close.
There's a silent communication
always taking place within
their minds and hearts.
They communicate much
while speaking few words.
They sense within their spirits
when the other is in need.
They know when to reach out
and when to stay away.
They know when to speak out
and when to remain silent.
Friends, no matter how far apart they are,
can stay close with few words,
as long as there is love in their hearts
for each other.

■ Sherrie L. Householder

Together, We've Made It Through a Lot

Laugh and the world laughs with you. Cry and you cry with your girlfriends.

■ Laurie Kuslansky

Girlfriends are those women who know us better than anyone (sometimes better than we know ourselves). They are not only essential for coping with our day-to-day frustrations or sharing private jokes, they help us limp through a crisis and, in the long run, help us grow as women and human beings.

■ Carmen Renee Berry and Tamara Traeder

The friend who holds your hand and says the wrong thing is made of dearer stuff than the one who stays away.

■ Barbara Kingsolver

She was there when I got married and she was there when I got divorced and she was there when my children were born.... We're very, very close.

■ Gayle King

Girlfriends
Keep Us Sane

Girlfriends are all ears when we need them to listen. They lend us a hand if we need their help. They're generous, and they'll give us the shirts off their backs if they know we want them. They're fun to hang out with, talk silly about nothing with, shop with, and cheat on our diets with.

They understand our feelings and show us acceptance and perspective. They acknowledge our efforts when we're trying hard. They help relieve the pressure of everyday life just by always being there.

What would we do without our girlfriends
to complain to and act so crazy with?
They're sensitive to our moods, and they
stand by us when we need them to. They
lend us their shoulders to cry on. They
laugh with us when life's not all that funny
and we get caught in some mess. They lift
us and encourage us and support us. They're
our refuge in this unfriendly world, our
buddies to walk with through the storms.
Girlfriends keep us sane.

■ Donna Fargo

You've Got to Have Friends

Whether we manage children and husbands, or professions and investments, we have always needed to connect with other women. From the playground to the end of our lives, our female friendships often form the foundation of our lives and an invaluable part of our support system.

■ Annette Annechild, PhD

Some people go to priests; others to poetry; I to my friends.

■ Virginia Woolf

You've got to have friends. Real ones. The kind you can call at 2:35 a.m. to meet you at the hospital or pick you up at the station. Friends who will pour peppermint tea while you pour out your heart and who will never once say, "I told you so!" Old friends who know where you've been and new friends who can see where you're headed. You simply must have one friend who can help you ask the questions without needing to know the answers. You can have a soul mate and a life partner and a spouse and a mother and a sister. But even then, you've got to have friends.

■ Rachel Snyder

Girlfriends Are Always There

A girlfriend says,
   "I'll be there for you..."
      and is.
A girlfriend says,
   "I care about you..."
      and does.
A girlfriend says,
   "You are important to me..."
      and means it.
A girlfriend says,
   "Call me when you need me..."
      and answers when you do.
A girlfriend says,
   "If you need anything,
      let me know..."
         and gives.

Thank you for being
that kind of girlfriend to me.

■ Doreen Stewart

You are the one person
who shares my deepest thoughts
and loves me in spite of them.
You rally behind me in my good decisions
and are there to help me through
	the consequences of the bad ones.
Who else can I call at any hour
	of the day or night?
Who else accepts and understands all of me?
No matter what comes along, good or bad,
	you'll be there.
It brings me great comfort
to know that I can always count on you.
I hope you know
I am that same sort of friend to you.
Our secrets are safe and our hearts
	are protected
because of the bond between us...
two special friends.
	■ Pamela Malone-Melton

Promises Between Girlfriends

I promise that I'll thank every wishing star that ever shined for bringing your closeness and understanding to me.

I promise that nothing will ever change the amount of appreciation I have for you. I promise that if I ever have news to share, you'll always be first on the call list. I promise if I ever release a genie from a magic lamp, I'll share my three wishes with you. In the event that never happens, I promise that you're welcome to split any pizza I might have in my possession. (And the same goes for chocolate.)

I promise I will be there to see you through anything that tries to get you down. I promise that I'll be around through it all, I'll support you in your efforts, and I'll believe in you at all times. We'll do whatever it takes, and together we'll chase away the clouds and keep the sun shining in our lives. When you need to be around someone who truly appreciates your crazy sense of humor, I will gladly, happily, and joyfully be that person.

I'll never take the beauty of our friendship for granted, and I'll never stop trying to tell you how much you mean to me.

I promise.

■ L. N. Mallory

Being a Fabulous Friend to Ourselves and Others: A Manifesto

- Through spirit, we provide a wide and deep resting place for each other. We challenge each other gently and firmly when necessary

- In joy and pleasure we dedicate our energy and time

- We are teachers for each other and use a wide-angle lens for seeing love

- We celebrate our successes and acknowledge when we feel jealous

■ We stand close in grief-times and allow tremendous love to fill the empty places

■ We recognize and acknowledge growth especially if and when our friend can't see it

■ We find value in our regular days and shine a bright light on simple kindness

■ We hold our friendship in sacred holy space, especially through humor, lightness, and exploration

■ We listen and speak with whole hearts whenever possible

■ SARK

Girlfriends Believe in Each Other's Dreams

Just knowing that my friend believes in me gives me confidence to go after my dreams. If I fail, she'll be there to comfort me and inspire me to try again. If I succeed, she'll delight in my achievement as much as if it were her own. Either way, I'll grow... and so will our friendship.

■ April Weston

Another way female friends help us grow is by accompanying us in activities that stretch us, developing and expressing new sides of ourselves. Whether it's training for a marathon, learning Spanish, picking up watercolor painting, or going back to graduate school, these new steps produce more pleasure and less anxiety taken in tandem. Even if a friend doesn't join us, she's likely to do the next best thing — encourage us and applaud our progress.

■ Sandy Sheehy

We have formed
a friendship
that has become
invaluable to me
We discuss our goals
and plan our future
We express our fears
and talk about our dreams
We can be very serious
or we can just have fun
We understand each other's lives
and try to encourage each other
in all that we do
We have formed
a friendship
that makes our lives
so much
nicer

■ Susan Polis Schutz

You Inspire Me, My Friend

Your special blend of caring goes a long
way toward proving there are still kindhearted
people in this world — people who seem
to receive their greatest joy by sharing the
best of themselves with others.

■ Cindy Chuksudoon

You can do certain things better than
anyone else I know. You make mistakes,
but you get past them. You know what it
means to live and learn and grow. You are
your own person. You've got your own
way of doing things, making things, and
getting through things... and you inspire
me constantly.

■ Ashley Rice

$\mathcal{B}$ecause of you,
I have sunlight for my journey,
wings for my dreams,
and a lifetime of memories to cherish.
Because of you,
I have found my true happiness
and tasted life.
Because of your power,
I have light
and grace to guide my way.
Because of your laughter,
I have sunbeams and smiles
that dance in my heart.
Because of your wisdom,
I have found answers
where only problems once grew.
Because of you,
I have found a friendship
that means the world to me.

■ Linda E. Knight

Girl Talk

Female friendship is the one place
women can indulge in that particular
form of self-expression called girl talk.
Hair, makeup, clothes, diets, whether
a particular politician looks like she's
had a face-lift or a given male movie
star is too handsome to be attractive —
we would never venture into these
topics with a man.

◼ Sandy Sheehy

We talk, therefore we are... friends. Talk
can be serious or funny, painful or exuberant,
intense or joyous. But at the heart of the
connections made is one sentence that
women repeat over and over: "I know just
what you mean."

◼ Ellen Goodman and Patricia O'Brien

I love my husband, and I'd be lost without him. But I'd be at sea without my friends, too. Even if you're married to a fellow who's retired (or unemployed), you wouldn't dream of interrupting him 12 or 14 times a day to discuss and deconstruct the latest atrocity visited on you by boss or mother-in-law....

My friends are my touchstone, my sounding board, my reality check, my information source, and my solace — the best blend imaginable of Martha Stewart, Oprah, Mother Teresa, Betty Crocker, and Judge Judy. They have a way of telling the truth so it doesn't hurt too much. They have an infinite capacity to listen and listen and listen — even if they've heard the story hundreds of times before (and I can assure you they have).

They are also my best audience. I can't count the number of times a day that something happens — I'm flashing on a recent confrontation with the local butcher — and I think to myself, I can't wait to tell Arlene (or Lynn or Ann or Andrea). It's a slightly more mature version of the feeling I had when I was a teenager out on a date and thinking, I can't wait to call Jill (or Marilyn or Pam). It's almost as if the event hasn't really happened until I lay it out for my friends. It's like the sound of one hand clapping.

■ Joanne Kaufman

Friendship and Laughter
Go Hand in Hand

Wild laughter between friends is like music.

■ SARK

All I can tell you is that no one makes me laugh in my life more than my girlfriends.

■ Kathy Griffin

Shared laughter offers us pleasure during the fun times and a resilient strength during distress. Sometimes life just seems too ridiculous and unexplainable. Laughing by yourself in these times seems somehow bitter and mirthless, but... laughter shared with a friend feels sweet and healing.

■ Carmen Renee Berry and Tamara Traeder

$\mathcal{I}$n spite of all the things that have happened to me, we laugh every night about one thing or another. She absolutely keeps me grounded.

■ Oprah Winfrey

$\mathcal{W}$hoever said laughter is the best medicine was right — it's also the glue that holds friendships together. To laugh together at life's ridiculous turn of events makes those events bearable. To laugh at the funny things in life makes life wonderful. The real gift is having a friend to share... laughter with.

■ Ellen Jacob

Girlfriends Make Life More Fun

Sometimes we simply yearn for fun in our friendships. Our lives are so busy, so jammed with "oughts" and "shoulds," that the only way many of us can enjoy ourselves is to have a friend cajole us into joining her in some lighthearted pursuit....

With the right friend, we can recapture some of the zany delight we knew as little girls. We can ditch our responsible personas and be goofy and outrageous.

■ Sandy Sheehy

Technically, I guess,
we are not "girls" anymore —
but when my girlfriend and I get together,
that's what it feels like!
With her sense of humor
and the way she still loves to play,
she brings so much joy into my life.
I love the adventures we've had together,
and I look forward to all those
yet to come.

■ Karen Taylor-Good

Girlfriends Are
Forever

When we are old women
we will sit on the porch
and watch the leaves tremble
in autumn's breath
We will rock on rocking chairs —
the lull of aged wood
creaking under our feet
We will wear pretty dresses
with yellow flowers in our hair
and hum songs in our heads
to the beat of children's laughter
in the distance

We will say nothing at times
and that silence will be
our greatest solace
Other times we will talk for hours
or until the sun sinks into night
and the moon comes out to play
We will remember then
the days when life was defined
by complexity
when we danced in the moonlight
until the sun came out
and when we vowed our friendship
would last a lifetime

■ Deana Marino

Thank You...

For being there for me always
and letting me know my
thoughts, feelings, and heart
are forever safe with you.

For letting me know I can
come to you with anything
and be offered both
comfort and space.

For cheering me on in my victories
and reassuring me that no matter
what a scoreboard or circumstance says,
I can never truly be defeated.

For having faith in me
without fail
and letting me know
that whatever else
may be going on around me,
I always have a friend in you.

Thank you
for being such a wonderful woman.
I appreciate you with all my heart
for the loving difference
you've made in my life.

■ Lynn Keachie

What I Wish for You, My Friend...

I wish you blue skies and a peaceful heart... a long and happy life... confidence to listen to the voice that speaks to you from within... courage to follow your dreams... understanding for the times when you stray from your path... the chance to be everything you want to be... whatever material and intangible wealth you need... work that is fulfilling and satisfying... permission to forgive yourself if you should ever fall short of your goals... great successes in life that come at times that are most meaningful for you.

I wish for you, my friend... a place where you can live in harmony with nature and the rest of the world... magical nights... fun and excitement each day... serenity... people who care deeply about you... and whom you care about, too... memories of times and places that will always remain close to your heart... wishes made on stars that eventually come true... knowledge of what a dear and exceptional friend you are to me... that all these special wishes will someday unfold for you.

■ Anna Marie Edwards

You Will Always Be
Just like a Sister to Me

A girlfriend is the one person on this earth
you feel whole with, the one you share who
you really are with.

She knows where you're coming from,
all you've been through,
and everything you're dreaming about.
She is the one you tell anything to,
ask anything of, and do anything for.

She is the one you tell all your truths to,
the one you give your whole heart to.
She is absolute acceptance,
abiding affection, and unconditional caring.
Just spending a moment with her
chases your cares away
and puts a smile on your face.

A girlfriend is the one who believes in you,
who accepts you and respects you,
the one you can call on anytime,
the one who never lets you down.
A girlfriend fills a unique space in your life.
She's a piece of your very heart and soul
and because of her you know without a doubt
that love can get you through anything.

I'm so blessed to have found in you
my friend of a lifetime,
my girlfriend, my best friend,
a sister I choose.

— Vickie M. Worsham

Acknowledgments continued...